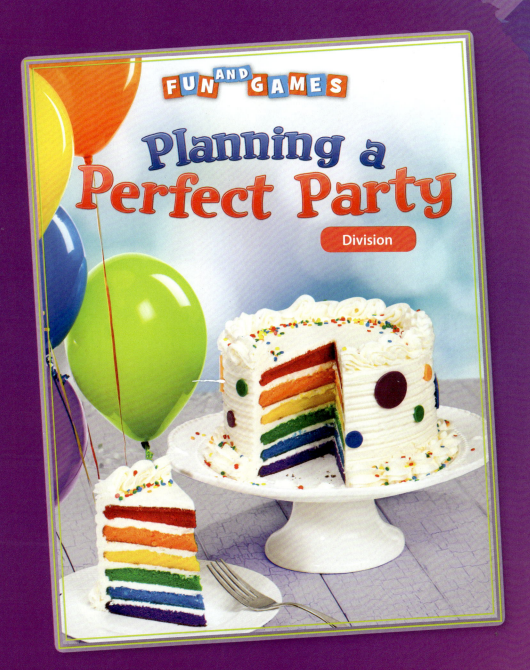

## Consultants

**Michele Ogden, Ed.D**
Principal, Irvine Unified School District

**Jennifer Robertson, M.A.Ed.**
Teacher, Huntington Beach City School District

## Publishing Credits

Rachelle Cracchiolo, M.S.Ed., *Publisher*
Conni Medina, M.A.Ed., *Managing Editor*
Dona Herweck Rice, *Series Developer*
Emily R. Smith, M.A.Ed., *Series Developer*
Diana Kenney, M.A.Ed., NBCT, *Content Director*
Stacy Monsman, M.A., *Editor*
Kevin Panter, *Graphic Designer*

**Image Credits:** p. 8 The Party Shoppe, LLC www.thepartyshoppe.net; 26 Burke/Triolo Productions/Getty Images; all other images from iStock and/or Shutterstock.

**Library of Congress Cataloging-in-Publication Data**

Names: McKissick, Katie.
Title: Fun and games : planning a perfect party / Katie McKissick.
Other titles: Planning a perfect party
Description: Huntington Beach, CA : Teacher Created Materials, [2017] | Audience: K to grade 3. | Includes index.
Identifiers: LCCN 2016053329 (print) | LCCN 2017008288 (ebook) | ISBN 9781480757998 (pbk.) | ISBN 9781480758636 (eBook)
Subjects: LCSH: Birthday parties--Juvenile literature.
Classification: LCC GV1472.7.B5 M35 2017 (print) | LCC GV1472.7.B5 (ebook) |
 DDC 793.2/1--dc23
LC record available at https://lccn.loc.gov/2016053329

### Teacher Created Materials

5301 Oceanus Drive
Huntington Beach, CA 92649-1030
http://www.tcmpub.com

**ISBN 978-1-4807-5799-8**
© 2018 Teacher Created Materials, Inc.

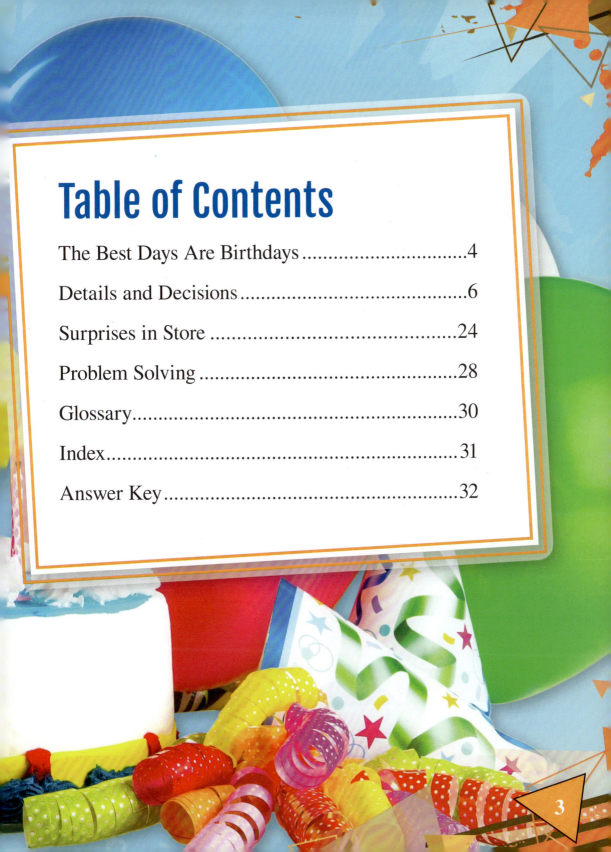

# Table of Contents

The Best Days Are Birthdays ...................................4

Details and Decisions ..............................................6

Surprises in Store ...................................................24

Problem Solving .....................................................28

Glossary ..................................................................30

Index .......................................................................31

Answer Key ............................................................32

# The Best Days Are Birthdays

Malika loves birthdays. They are always a lot of fun! When her friends have birthday parties, she can't wait to go. She looks forward to the games and the food. But, her favorite part is talking with her friends about the terrific party they just attended! Malika wants to be sure that her party gives everyone plenty to talk about.

Malika's party is just two weeks away. So, she is giving it a lot of thought. She wants to **include** all of her friends. There have to be decorations. Games are important, too. Tasty food is a must! Malika realizes this birthday party will take **effort**. She has to **plan** it all out, and there is no time to lose. She wants her party to be special because her friends are special. After all, a birthday party only happens once a year. She wants everyone to remember hers.

Guest lists help party planners make sure everyone has been invited.

# Details and Decisions

It's time to get to work! Planning a party takes time and thought. There are many **details** to consider. Malika is ready, though. She has some great ideas for putting together a wonderful birthday party for herself and her friends.

There are a lot of **decisions** to make. First, she needs to decide what decorations there should be. Then, she needs to figure out how many of the decorations she will need.

Calendars and checklists help people track time and tasks when planning big events.

Next, she needs to decide how many people to invite. This part is important. She wants to have all of her friends come to her party. When she knows how many people will be there, she can start planning the food. What would a birthday party be without food? It would be a lot of hungry people!

Last, she needs to think about party **favors**. It is fun to leave a birthday with a little present. She wants her guests to feel special, too.

This party store sells latex and mylar balloons.

# Decorations

Malika wants her party to be bright and exciting. She thinks back to her friend Jin's birthday party. There were balloons everywhere she looked. It was very pretty. She decides she wants her party to look like that, too.

At the party store, Malika finds the balloon **aisle**. But there are so many! They are different sizes and colors. There are balloons made of latex, which is like rubber. There are balloons made of mylar, which is like foil. Malika has some hard decisions to make.

Malika likes the plain latex balloons the best. But she can't decide which color to get. She thinks about it for a long time. Finally, she picks the yellow and blue balloons. Those are her favorite colors. She plans to tie them in groups around her house.

Malika thinks the colors will look great. But she does not know how many balloons to buy. She wants them to be equally **divided** among the 5 tables at her party. She sees a bag of 15 balloons. Since there are 5 tables, that means there will be 3 balloons at each table.

That seems nice, but Malika wants something special! Maybe there should be 5 balloons on each table. This means she needs more than 15. So, she **multiplies**. She knows that she has 5 tables. Now, she knows the number of balloons she wants at each.

Placing 5 balloons on each of the 5 tables means there will be 25 balloons. Malika sees a package of 10 blue balloons. Next to it is a bag with 10 yellow balloons. Finally, she sees a package of 5 sparkly silver balloons. This is perfect! She has the right number of balloons for her party.

## LET'S EXPLORE MATH

1. The party store has 24 balloons and 3 displays. If each display has an equal number of balloons, how many balloons does each display have?

2. What if the store sets up one more display? How many balloons would each display have now?

This cake could not feed 400 people.

# Invitations

Now it is time to start thinking about guests. Malika needs to send invitations. But first, she must decide how many people to invite.

She gives the guest list a lot of thought. She needs to plan well. She wants to invite all of her friends, but she can't invite everyone she knows. She imagines a party with everyone from her school. That would be 400 people! A party that big would be crazy. There wouldn't be enough room for everyone. Her house certainly wouldn't have enough chairs. She would also have to buy a lot of food and cake. Buying that much food would be expensive; much more expensive than what her current **budget** allows. And there's no way that 400 guests could share the food that she could afford to buy. Who would enjoy a **sliver** of cake or a pinch of party mix?

Next, Malika imagines a party with just her family. Family parties can be fun. She had one last year. At that party, they all ate food and sang. But they didn't really play any games. Malika decides to share a fun celebration with her friends.

Malika thinks about her **options**. Now, she has to make a decision. She knows she can't invite her whole school. She also knows she wants to invite more than just family members. Her class has 20 students. That number sounds about right. She has enough money in her budget to buy food for 20 people. And, since she can invite everyone in her class, no one will feel left out. Malika decides this is the perfect plan.

## LET'S EXPLORE MATH

1. Malika wants to use stickers to decorate her invitations. A package of 42 stickers is labeled: "Enough to decorate 7 invitations." If Malika puts the same number of stickers on each invitation, how many stickers can she put on each?

2. Malika changes her mind and decides to use the stickers to decorate only 6 invitations. If Malika puts the same number of stickers on each invitation, how many stickers can she put on each?

## Food

Malika is almost done planning her party. She has invited students from her class. She has picked decorations. Now, it is time to think about food. But, food is tricky. People like different things. Malika doesn't have to think about this long. Her favorite food is pizza, and that's what she wants to serve.

How much pizza should she order? Malika has to decide. But she's not worried. She knows how many people are coming, so this will be easy.

There are two ways Malika can plan. She can order a lot of pizza and divide it among the 20 people. She can also guess how many slices of pizza each person will eat and multiply that by 20. Both ways will work.

Malika decides she needs 40 slices of pizza. If she divides those slices among the 20 people at the party, each person will have 2 slices. That seems right to Malika. She can now cross one more item off her list!

## LET'S EXPLORE MATH

1. Malika wonders if 2 slices each is enough. She changes her mind and decides she wants each guest to have 3 slices of pizza. How many slices of pizza does she need now?

2. A large pizza comes with 10 slices. How many large pizzas will Malika need to order if each guest gets 3 slices?

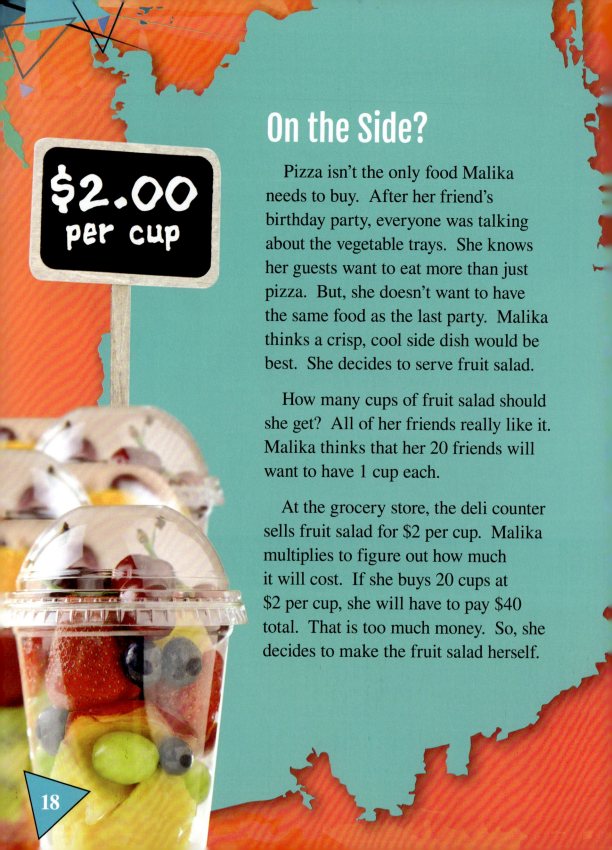

## On the Side?

Pizza isn't the only food Malika needs to buy. After her friend's birthday party, everyone was talking about the vegetable trays. She knows her guests want to eat more than just pizza. But, she doesn't want to have the same food as the last party. Malika thinks a crisp, cool side dish would be best. She decides to serve fruit salad.

How many cups of fruit salad should she get? All of her friends really like it. Malika thinks that her 20 friends will want to have 1 cup each.

At the grocery store, the deli counter sells fruit salad for $2 per cup. Malika multiplies to figure out how much it will cost. If she buys 20 cups at $2 per cup, she will have to pay $40 total. That is too much money. So, she decides to make the fruit salad herself.

## LET'S EXPLORE MATH

Fruit is on sale at the grocery store. Malika can buy a bag of mixed fruit that has 5 cups for $5.

1. How many bags of mixed fruit will Malika need if she still wants 20 cups?
2. How much will 1 cup of mixed fruit cost?
3. How much will 20 cups of mixed fruit cost?

**$5.00 per bag**

# Party Favors

It is almost time for Malika's party! All that is left to do is sort the party favors. Malika is excited for this task. She wants to thank her guests for coming. And, she has a lot of fun things to give her friends.

| Party Favors | Number |
|---|---|
| marbles | 100 |
| paddleballs | 20 |
| pencils | 40 |
| bubbles | 20 |
| bags | 20 |

Malika counts 20 colorful bags. Malika wants each bag to have the same number of items. It will not be fair for some people to get more than others.

Malika has marbles, pencils, paddleballs, and bubbles. First, she figures out how many favors she has. But she keeps losing count! Malika decides to keep a list. She counts the marbles and writes 100. Next, she counts the paddleballs and writes 20.

Malika is running out of time and needs to get the favors into the bags quickly. She starts with her pile of marbles. Since she wants each bag to have the same number of marbles, she decides to use division.

Malika has 100 marbles and 20 bags. That means she can put 5 marbles into each bag. She splits them into groups of 5. Next, she moves on to the paddleballs. There are 20 bags and 20 paddleballs. So, each bag gets 1.

Malika hopes her friends will enjoy the party favors. She tried to choose favors that everyone will like. She can't wait for people to start arriving!

# LET'S EXPLORE MATH

Malika continues counting her party favors and finishes writing her list.

1. How many bottles of bubbles will be in each bag?
2. How many pencils can Malika place in each bag?
3. Malika wants to make extra party favor bags with wind-up toys for her younger cousins who can't come to the party. She has 30 wind-up toys and wants to put 6 in each bag. How many bags can she fill?
4. What if she puts 5 wind-up toys in each bag? Now how many bags can she fill?

| Party Favors | Number |
|---|---|
| marbles | 100 |
| paddleballs | 20 |
| pencils | 40 |
| bubbles | 20 |
| bags | 20 |

## Surprises in Store

The day has finally arrived…it's party time! Malika is so excited. There are balloons everywhere, and her friends have come. They are eating pizza and playing games. The party favor bags are all lined up on the table. Malika is thankful that she can share her special day with her friends.

But then, there is a really big surprise! Someone brought friends from out of town. There are 4 more people at the party. Malika planned for exactly 20 people, and now there are 24. What should she do? Should she ask them to leave? That would be an uncomfortable conversation. And Malika doesn't want to be rude. There must be a way to include them. Malika tries to think of a plan. She wants to make sure everyone gets to have some of the delicious pizza. How can she make sure that happens?

Malika thought she was going to have 20 guests. She ordered 6 large pizzas so each person could have 3 slices. That was a total of 60 slices of pizza. But now, that might not be enough.

Malika sees that some of her guests are only eating 2 slices of pizza. Maybe there will be enough for the new friends.

Malika tries to count the number of guests only eating 2 slices. But they all keep moving around! She decides to count the number of pizza slices still on the table. Malika estimates that the 4 new people will each eat 3 slices of pizza. If there are 12 slices left, Malika won't have to order more!

## LET'S EXPLORE MATH

Imagine Malika decides to order extra pizza. She needs 12 more slices. A small pizza has 4 slices. How many small pizzas should she order?

# Problem Solving

Liam is a guest at Malika's party. He is very excited. There are many games to play and things to do. It's hard to decide which one to do first. To help guests choose how to spend their time, a table has been posted. It shows how long each activity takes. Find out how Liam plans his time at the party by answering the questions.

1. Liam will be at the party for 45 minutes. How many times can he go in the bounce house?

2. Liam visits the bounce house twice. Next, he has his face painted. Does he have enough time to change his mind and have his face repainted?

3. Liam has 30 minutes before he has to leave. How many times can he complete the obstacle course? Will he have any time left?

4. Liam spends an equal number of minutes on each obstacle. How many obstacles could there be in the obstacle course? How many minutes can he spend on each?

| Activity | Time Required |
|---|---|
| obstacle course | 9 minutes |
| face painting | 15 minutes |
| bounce house | 5 minutes |

# Glossary

**aisle**—space with shelves on both sides where people walk through a store

**budget**—a plan for using money over a period of time

**decisions**—choices you make

**details**—small parts of things

**divided**—shared or grouped into equal parts

**effort**—energy used to do something

**favors**—small gifts given at parties

**include**—to make someone or something a part of something else

**multiplies**—adds a number to itself multiple times

**options**—choices or possibilities

**plan**—to think about the details of something before it happens

**sliver**—a very thin piece that has been cut, broken, or torn from something larger

# Index

balloons, 9–11, 24

cost, 18–19

decisions, 6, 9

decorations, 4, 6, 9, 16

details, 6

divided, 10, 16

equally, 10, 29

food, 4, 7, 13–14, 16, 18

games, 4, 14, 24, 28

guests, 7, 13, 18, 20, 26, 28

multiplies, 10, 16, 18

pizza, 16–18, 24, 26–27

plan, 4, 6, 7, 9, 13–14, 16, 24, 28

# Answer Key

## Let's Explore Math

**page 11:**
1. 8 balloons
2. 6 balloons

**page 15:**
1. 6 stickers
2. 7 stickers

**page 17:**
1. 60 slices
2. 6 pizzas

**page 19:**
1. 4 bags
2. $1
3. $20

**page 23:**
1. 1 bottle
2. 2 pencils
3. 5 bags
4. 6 bags

**page 27:**
3 small pizzas

## Problem Solving

1. 9 times
2. Yes, Liam will have enough time because 10 + 15 + 15 = 40, which is less than the 45 minutes he has left at the party.
3. 3 times; 3 minutes left
4. 1 obstacle, 9 minutes; 3 obstacles, 3 minutes each; 9 obstacles, 1 minute each